My First Animal Library

Tigers

by Cari Meister

Bullfrog Books

Ideas for Parents and Teachers

Bullfrog Books let children practice reading informational text at the earliest reading levels. Repetition, familiar words, and photo labels support early readers.

Before Reading

- Discuss the cover photo. What does it tell them?

- Look at the picture glossary together. Read and discuss the words.

Read the Book

- "Walk" through the book and look at the photos. Let the child ask questions. Point out the photo labels.

- Read the book to the child, or have him or her read independently.

After Reading

- Prompt the child to think more. Ask: Have you seen a tiger before? Where did you see it? Was it hiding in some tall grass at the zoo?

Bullfrog Books are published by Jump!
5357 Penn Avenue South
Minneapolis, MN 55419
www.jumplibrary.com

Library of Congress Cataloging-in-Publication Data

Meister, Cari, author.
 Tigers / by Cari Meister.
    pages cm. — (Bullfrog books.
My first animal library)
 Audience: Age 5.
 Audience: K to grade 3.
 Includes index.
 ISBN 978-1-62031-169-1 (hardcover) —
 ISBN 978-1-62496-256-1 (ebook)
 1. Tiger—Juvenile literature. I. Title.
QL737.C23M456 2015
599.756—dc23
                                    2014032122

Series Editor: Wendy Dieker
Series Designer: Ellen Huber
Book Designer: Anna Peterson
Photo Researcher: Jenny Fretland VanVoorst

Photo Credits: All photos by Shutterstock except: Corbis, 12–13; Dreamstime, 10; Nature Picture Library, 14–15.

Printed in the United States of America at Corporate Graphics in North Mankato, Minnesota.

Table of Contents

A Good Hunter

Shh! A tiger hunts.

He stalks his prey.

He has stripes.

They help him blend in.

No two tigers have the same stripes.

The tiger hides.

The deer does not see him.

prey

11

The tiger runs.

He has strong legs.

He is fast.

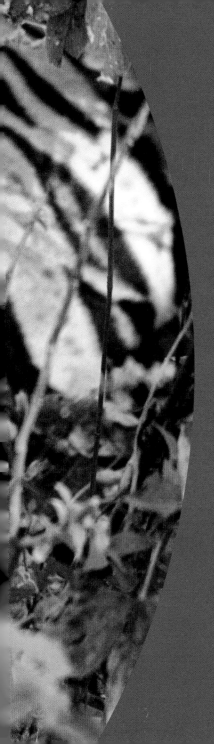

The tiger grabs the deer with his sharp teeth.

Now he can eat.

He will eat some now.

He will save some
for later.

The tiger washes his face.

He uses
his paws.

19

It is a hot day.

The tiger needs to cool off.

He goes for a swim.

Splash!

Parts of a Tiger

fur
Striped fur helps tigers hide.

tail
A tiger uses its tail for balance and to talk to other tigers.

claws
Tigers have retractable claws. That means they can make their claws go into their paws or make them stick out.

Picture Glossary

blend in
To match things around it and to be hard to see.

stalk
To follow by moving quietly.

prey
Animals that are hunted by another animal.

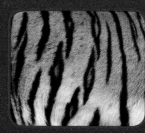

stripes
Long lines.

Index

To Learn More

Learning more is as easy as 1, 2, 3.

1) Go to www.factsurfer.com

2) Enter "tigers" into the search box.

3) Click the "Surf" button to see a list of websites.

With factsurfer.com, finding more information is just a click away.